HOW TO BUILD AN AK 47

By
MARSHALL TRIVETT

COPYRIGHT © 2022 - MARSHALL TRIVETT
All rights reserved.

Contents

Introduction
Short History and Description 2
What Are the Legal Aspects? 3
    Summary of Federal Regulatory Requirements 6
    Some State and Local Municipalities Have Far Stricter Requirements 7
Planning the Task 7
    Selecting Tools 7
    Choosing a Parts Kit 8
Taking the Old AK Apart 10
    Disassemble the Kit 11
    Field-Strip the Weapon 11
        Breaking the Weapon Down 12
        …..And now the hard part…. 13
        …..And now the tricky part…. 15
    Cleaning Parts 16
        Removing the Crud from Metal Parts 16
        Removing the Wood from the Upper Handguard 17
    Refinishing the Wooden Parts 17
    Refinishing the Metal Parts 18
What to Discard 19
To Buy or Build Your Receiver 20
    Building Your Receiver 21
Reassembly of the Major Assemblies 22
    Reinstalling the Barrel 22
    Reinstalling the Remaining Barrel Assemblies 23
    Reassembly of the Receiver 25
        Installing the Receiver (Trunnion) Blocks 25
    Installing the Trigger Assembly 27
    Final Rifle Reassembly 28

Introduction

This manual provides the necessary instructions for a law-abiding U.S. citizen with a reasonable amount of mechanical skill to procure the materials and build a semiautomatic Kalashnikov Type 47 assault rifle.

A once avid hunter and retired U.S. Army Reserve Officer, I undertook this effort because I found the subject fascinating, and I have been a firearms enthusiast all my life. Firearms are tools for hunting, sporting competition, self-defense, and war. They are not to be feared, but they should be respected. Having this perspective on firearms is not difficult to understand since I was raised in a relatively rural part of Texas, where it was common to see rifles sitting in the back window gun racks of half the pickups in the high school parking lot. Weapons on a school campus did not raise any eyebrows in my town in the mid-seventies. Unfortunately, the world has changed and become a far more dangerous place. That said, I do not feel that only criminals should be the owners of capable firearms, producing a relatively comprehensive instruction manual for building your AK47.

In the hands of a disciplined marksman, the semiautomatic AK47 is an exceptionally capable weapon within the 200-yard engagement range. The AK47 can consistently produce an inch or inch and a half grouping at 100 yards without special sights. However, this should not deter most hunters (or, for that matter, most soldiers) for two reasons: 1) rarely does one get many wild game shots in wooded or brushy areas beyond 100 yards, and 2) it is difficult to make positive target identification (animal, friendly, or enemy soldier) beyond 300 yards (with optical assistance). Therefore, you don't need a weapon to engage targets at ranges they cannot be seen, or if they can be seen, they cannot be adequately identified.

Unlike the higher velocity (lower mass) 5.56mm (.223 caliber), common to the M16/AR15, the 7.62mm has more physical momentum when it hits the target, especially when the round strikes the target at something other than perpendicular angles. Any soldier that has observed 5.56 rounds deflect off a car's windshield in combat knows what I mean.

However, the fact that 7.62 x39mm ammunition can presently be purchased in bulk for around .25¢ a round (sometimes less) makes it an ideal weapon for shooters with a budget.

Chapter 1: Where to Start?

Short History and Description

The Kalashnikov Type 47 assault rifle, also known as the AK 47, was first officially accepted by the Soviet Armed Forces in 1949 and eventually used by most of the member states of the Warsaw Pact.

The World War II German, Sturmgewehr 44 (*aka, "storm" or "assault" rifle model 44, Maschinenpistole 44, MP 44*) was the first true "assault rifle." Patterned after the Sturmgewehr and built by the Soviets shortly after World War II, the AK 47 has become the most widely adopted and produced assault rifle ever made. The AK's durability, low production cost, and simplicity of operation have resulted in its being manufactured in many countries worldwide.

These weapons had many similarities; they both possessed an effective range of 3 to 400 meters, were relatively light, easy to handle, capable of semi and full-auto rates of fire, produced from a sheet metal stamping process, and therefore inexpensive to manufacture.

The Sturmgewehr 44 rifle was chambered for the 7.92×33mm cartridge.

Figure 1 - Sturmgewehr 44

Figure 2 - AK47

However, the AK47 rifle was initially chambered for a slightly smaller projectile and higher velocity (and larger) 7.62×39mm cartridge.

Now that we have familiarized ourselves with some of the history and attributes of the AK47, let's get to the task of building one.

Chapter 1: Where to Start?

Below is an outline of what you will learn in this chapter. All chapters begin with a similar outline.
- ✓ What are the *legal aspects* associated with building firearms?
- ✓ Summary of Federal Regulatory Requirements
- ✓ Some State and Local Municipalities Have Far Stricter Requirements
- ✓ Planning the Task
- ✓ Parts Kits
- ✓ Selecting Tools

 *Note: Be aware that essential facts and cautionary information are pointed out throughout the text with small "AK47s" ( ) depicted in the left-hand margin.*

 *Note: When going through the instructions, read the whole chapter before starting the task to ensure you do not skip the required precautionary notes, which may cause damage, rework, or injury.*

What Are the Legal Aspects?

Before starting a task, whether adding a *new addition to your house* or *building a rifle*, it is always good practice to investigate the regulatory and legal restrictions associated with the undertaking. Federal, State, and sometimes local restrictions are associated with buying, selling, manufacturing, and even owning firearms.

I have researched the Federal Regulatory requirements and have included them below. I have not included the state and local requirements because it varies from locality to locality, and that is something you will have to do for yourself.

Chapter 1: Where to Start?

I have included the Federal Regulatory requirements for your review to understand better the whys behind several of the steps I have included in the following planning and assembly instructions. The key aspects of the pertinent regulations are called out in **bold** font.
The following are excerpts from the Alcohol, Tobacco, and Firearms website. I encourage you to follow the link provided and verify the Federal Regulations for yourself.
(http://www.atf.gov/firearms/faq/firearms-technology.html#commercial-parts-assembly):

Per provisions of the Gun Control Act (G.C.A.) of 1968, 18 U.S.C. Chapter 44, **an unlicensed individual may make a "firearm"** as defined in the G.C.A. for personal use **but not for sale or distribution.**

Per 18 USC 5845 ... The term "firearm" means: (1) a shotgun having a barrel or barrels of less than 18 inches in length; (2) a weapon made from a shotgun if such weapon as modified has an overall length of less than 26 inches or a barrel or barrels of less than 18 inches in length; (3, **a rifle having a barrel or barrels of less than 16 inches in length**; (4) **a weapon made from a rifle if such weapon as modified has an overall length of less than 26 inches or a barrel or barrels of less than 16 inches in length;** (5) any other weapon, as defined in 18 USC 5845 (e); (6) a machinegun; (7) a muffler or a silencer for any firearm whether or not such firearm is included within this definition; and (8) a destructive device.

The G.C.A., 18 U.S.C. § 921(a)(3), defines the term "firearm" to include the following:

.... (A) any weapon (including a starter gun) which will or is designed to or may be readily converted to expel a projectile by the action of an explosive: (B) the frame or receiver of any such weapon; (C) any firearm muffler or silencer; or (D) any destructive device. Such a term does not include an antique firearm.

....generally an **unlicensed person cannot manufacture a machine gun**. However, if documentation can be provided, along with the Application to Make a Machinegun, which establishes that the weapon is being made for distribution to a Federal or State agency, an individual may be permitted to make the machine gun. [18 U.S.C. 922(o)(2), 27 CFR 479.105(e)]

In addition, the National Firearms Act (NFA), 26 U.S.C. § 5845(b), defines the term "**machinegun**" as:

... any weapon which shoots, is designed to shoot, or can be readily restored to **shoot, automatically more than one shot, without manual reloading, by a single function of the trigger**. This term shall also include the frame or receiver of any such weapon, any part designed and intended solely and exclusively, or combination of parts designed and intended, for use in converting a weapon into a machinegun, and any combination of parts from which a machinegun can be assembled if such parts are in the possession or under the control of a person.

Finally, the G.C.A., 18 U.S.C. § 922(r), specifically states the following:

Chapter 1: Where to Start?

It shall be **unlawful for any person to assemble from imported parts any semiautomatic rifle or any shotgun which is identical to any rifle or shotgun prohibited from importation** under the...[G.C.A.]...Section 925(d)(3).as not being particularly suitable for or readily adaptable to sporting purposes ....

Also, 27 C.F.R. § 478.39 states:

... (a) **No person shall assemble a semiautomatic rifle or any shotgun using more than 10 of the imported parts listed in paragraph (c)** of this section if the assembled firearm is prohibited from importation under section 925(d)(3) as not being particularly suitable for or readily adaptable to sporting purposes ....

(b) The **provisions of this section shall not apply to**:

(1) The **assembly of such rifle or shotgun for sale or distribution by a licensed manufacturer** to the United States or any department or agency thereof or to any State or any department, agency, or political subdivision thereof; or (2) The **assembly of such rifle or shotgun for the purposes of testing or experimentation** authorized by the Director under the provisions of [§478.151(formerly 178.151)]; or (3) The **repair of any rifle or shotgun which had been imported into or assembled in the United States prior to November 30, 1990,** or the replacement of any part of such firearm.

(c) For purposes of this section, the term imported parts [tabulated below] are:
    (1) Frames, receivers, receiver castings, forgings, or castings.
    (2) Barrels.
    (3) Barrel extensions.
    (4) Mounting blocks (trunnions).
    (5) Muzzle attachments.
    (6) Bolts.
    (7) Bolt carriers.
    (8) Operating rods.
    (9) Gas pistons.
    (10) Trigger housings.
    (11) Triggers.
    (12) Hammers.
    (13) Sears.
    (14) Disconnectors.
    (15) Buttstocks.
    (16) Pistol grips.
    (17) Forearms, handguards.
    (18) Magazine bodies.
    (19) Followers.
    (20) Floor plates.

... As a result of a 1989 study by the U.S. Treasury Department regarding the importability of certain firearms, an import ban was placed on military-style firearms. This **ban included not**

only military-type firearms, but also extended to firearms with certain **features that were considered to be "nonsporting."**

Among such **nonsporting features** was the ability to accept a **detachable magazine, folding/telescoping stocks; separate pistol grips; and the ability to accept a bayonet, flash suppressors, bipods, grenade launchers, and night sights.**

Please note that the foreign parts kits that are sold through commercial means are usually cut up machineguns, such as Russian AK-47 types, British Sten types, etc. Generally, an acceptable semiautomatic copy of a machinegun is one that has been significantly redesigned. The **receiver must be incapable of accepting the original fire-control components that are designed to permit fully automatic fire**. The method of operation should employ a closed-bolt firing design that incorporates an inertia-type firing pin within the bolt assembly.

Further, an acceptably redesigned semiautomatic copy of a nonsporting firearm must be limited to **using less than 10 of the imported parts** listed in 27 C.F.R. § 478.39(c).

Otherwise, it is considered to be assembled into a nonsporting configuration per the provisions of 18 USC 925(d)(3) and is thus a violation of § 922(r).

 *Note: The 1989 Federal Assault Weapons Ban expired on September 13, 2004, as part of the law's sunset provision.*

Individuals manufacturing sporting-type firearms for their use need not hold Federal Firearms Licenses (FFLs). However, the A.T.F. suggests that the manufacturer at least identify the firearm with a **serial number as a safeguard in the event that the firearm is lost or stolen**. Also, the firearm should be identified as required in 27 CFR 478.92 if it is sold or otherwise lawfully transferred in the future.

Summary of Federal Regulatory Requirements

Bottom Line: In 1994, the "1989 Assault Weapons Ban" was allowed to expire. It is now legal to assemble a semi-auto AK-47 from a parts kit again as long as certain legalities are observed, such as a requirement that the certain U.S. manufactured pieces are used to substitute the imported ones.

 *Note: True AK-47 rifles are fully automatic; however, with the exception of Class-3 gun dealers, it is illegal to possess them in the U.S. However, the semi-auto variants, originating from imports with American manufactured receivers and parts attached, are about as close to owning a true AK-47 that most private citizens can achieve in most states.*

I have summarized the major controlling Federal Regulatory requirements that will affect you below:
- An unlicensed individual may make a "firearm" as defined in the G.C.A. for personal use but not for sale or distribution.
- An unlicensed individual cannot manufacture a machine gun.

Chapter 1: Where to Start?

- It is unlawful for any person to assemble from imported parts any semiautomatic rifle or any shotgun which is identical to any rifle or shotgun prohibited from importation.
- When you assemble your AK47, to be legal (per § 922(r)), it must have less than 10 of the imported parts listed in 27 C.F.R. § 478.39(c).
- The Barrel is 16" or longer, and the overall length is more than 26".

Lastly, it is not a Federal Regulatory requirement. Still, it is good practice to at least identify the firearm with a serial number as a safeguard if the firearm is lost or stolen.

Some State and Local Municipalities Have Far Stricter Requirements

Please note that Federal Law is not the legally guiding authority you must follow. Several states also have significant statutory requirements, including New York, California, and Massachusetts, to name a few.

New York, Massachusetts, and New Jersey states have enacted their *Assault Weapons Bans*. California was one of the first states to enact a ban on semiautomatic rifles in 1989; they have added stricter measures to the law several times since. Connecticut passed a partial ban that focuses on assault weapons with specific characteristics. Cook County, Illinois, also has enacted a similar but more restrictive assault weapons ban, and Washington DC (for all intents and purposes) does not allow privately owned firearms.

Planning the Task

To start, take a minute to outline your AK47 project. Your plan should begin with obtaining the tools you will need to disassemble and reassemble your weapon. Also, consider what type of rifle you want when you finish.

Selecting Tools

Before you get too far, be aware you will need a few tools to complete this task.

At the very minimum, you'll need:
- Hydraulic press (preferably 12-ton) available at "www.harborfreight.com"
- Drill Press
- Hammer and punch set
- Riveting jigs (the one shown is available at "ak-builder.com")
- Hand vice
- A Dremel® Tool comes in handy
- Various common hand tools (e.g., screwdrivers, hammers, etc.

Hydraulic Press

Riveting Jig

For an 80% receiver build, you'll also need:
- Flat bending jig
- Spot welder
- Propane torch
- Tap & die set (if you choose not to use rivets)

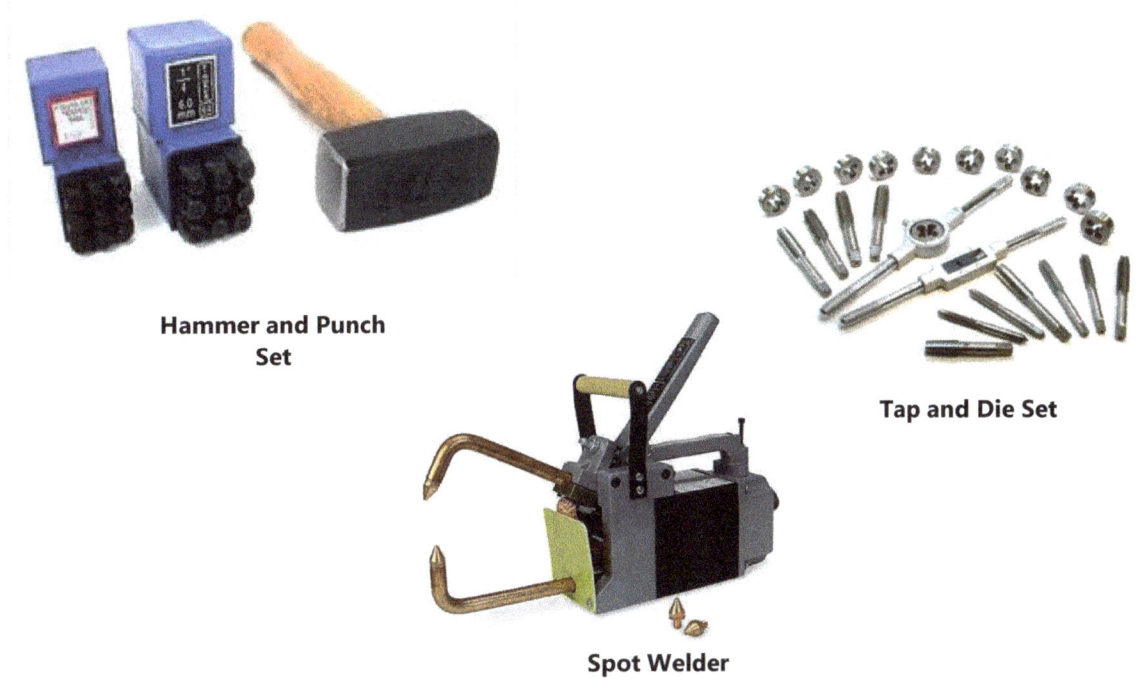

Hammer and Punch Set

Tap and Die Set

Spot Welder

Choosing a Parts Kit

A wide variety of Kalashnikov parts kits are available on the market. To obtain a listing, one only has to enter the "AK47 parts kit" into your internet browser's search engine. Before you choose one, do your homework. Begin by deciding which type of A.K. you want when the project is finished. To do this, ask yourself a few questions; What is the stock design I want? ….Folding? ….Wooden? Plastic?.... What caliber? 7.62?..... 5.56? After figuring out what style you want, go to a gun show and ask the dealers what they are looking for.

I recommend buying your kit at a gun show so that you can physically inspect the parts, but I know people who have had good luck buying their A.K. parts kits online. Some things to look for are:
- Age, wear, and corrosion;
- Bent or misshapen parts; and
- Parts should have the same lot number (otherwise, they may not fit during reassembly).

Chapter 1: Where to Start?

 *Note: At this point, you have realized that if you do not already own (or have a friend that will let you borrow) some of the more expensive tools required for this task (and you do not intend to build a significant number of AK47s that will assist in driving down costs) just purchasing the needed tools will make this project more expensive than simply buying a completed AK47 at a gun show or local gun store.*

 *Note: Assuming that you are not discouraged and still want to build your AK47, from a dematerialized kit, please proceed to Chapter 2, Parts Preparation.*

 *Note: A newly refurbished ready-to-fire AK 47, as of 2022, cost roughly $1000.*

 *Note: Below is a list of URLs where one can obtain demilitarized AK-47 parts kits and their respective prices as of summer 2022.*

- *https://armsofamerica.com/ $850 and up for a parts kit*
- *https://atlanticfirearms.com/ parts kits start at $600*
- *https://centerfiresystems.com/ parts kits start at $525*
- *https://whatacountry.com/ parts kits start at $550*
- *https://www.royaltigerimports.com/ parts kits start at $450*
- *https://www.apexgunparts.com/ parts kits start at $450*
- *https://sharpsbros.com/ parts kits start at $450*
- *https://max-arms.com/ parts kits start at $450*

Note: Some online firearms providers offer a barrel assembly version with all foreign metal refurbished and additional needed American parts for a reasonable price. The barrel assemblies generally only require the furniture to make the rifle complete. Furniture-Ready Barrel assemblies start at around $550.

- *https://palmettostatearmory.com/*
- *https://gun.deals/*

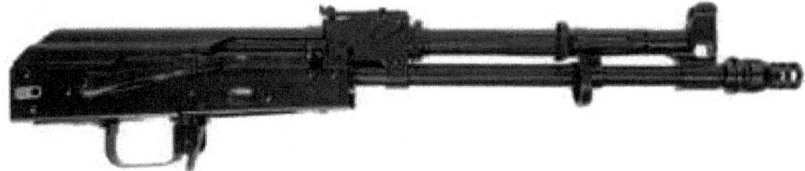

Furniture-Ready Barrel Assembly

Chapter 2: Parts Preparation

Below is an outline of what you will learn in this chapter.

Starting with the tools, parts, and materials you collected in the activities outlined in the previous chapter, we go through the disassembly and parts preparation of the original AK47.
- ✓ Disassembly of the old AK47.
- ✓ Cleaning the old parts.

Taking the Old AK Apart

At this point, you should have accumulated all required tools, materials, U.S. replacement parts, and a demilitarized A.K. parts kit for the type of weapon you desire to build. What you should have in front of you looks very similar to what is depicted in Figures 3 or 4.

Figure 3 displays an M85 Krinkov, the 5.56mm, carbine version of the A.K. built by the Yugoslavian government. Notice that the Barrel has already been removed, and the receiver is not part of the kit.

Chapter 2: Parts Preparation

Figure 3 - M85 Yugo "Krinkov"

Figure 4 - AK74 De-Militarized

In Figure 4 (AK 74), the Barrel is still attached, and the receiver assembly has been cut in half at an angle.

The steps you need to follow in disassembly will depend on what type of A.K. you choose, how it was demilitarized, and the parts that come with your kit.

Disassemble the Kit

The first step is to disassemble the kit. Some kits come fully disassembled (see Figure 3); if this is the case, go to the next step. If not (as shown in Figure 4), take everything out of the bag/box the kit came in, then inventory and inspect your kit.

Field-Strip the Weapon

The term *fieldstrip* is of military origin. It means to take apart (a weapon) for cleaning, lubrication, and repair or inspection. Your AK47 kit may already be fully broken-down to a *field-stripped* status. If not, I have included steps/instructions to ensure this is done before moving on to the more extensive disassembly requiring hand and power tools.

As you disassemble the weapon, discard the *full-auto trigger assembly* (if present). Use the *AK47 Parts Diagram* provided in this document to aid you in your inventory and inspection task. Take note of any defects, wear areas, corrosion, or missing parts.

 *Note: Using full-auto trigger parts are not legal.*

 *Note: As you move along, notice the instructions that follow; assume that you have the more traditional version of the AK47 (with the wooden stock). However, language has been inserted at critical points to address other models and types.*

 *Note: Refer to the exploded AK-47 Parts Diagram (for part names, numbers, and assembly orientation) provided in the text to aid you in the disassembly and assembly.*

Chapter 2: Parts Preparation

Breaking the Weapon Down

First, break the weapon down as far as you can by hand by removing:
- Receiver Cover (#63), depress the Recoil Spring Guide (#65), and lift the cover.
- Recoil Spring Assembly (part #s 65, 66, and 67), push forward until it clears the notch, then extract.
- Safety Lever (#68), rotate until perpendicular to the Receiver (#62), then extract sideways.
- If your kit has one, remove the Cleaning Rod (#16) by pulling down the tip (away from the Barrel) and sliding it out.
- The Bolt Carrier (#8) should be already removed; if not, remove it.
- Upper Handguard, Gas Cylinder (#80), lift the Handguard Latch (#81) until vertical and remove Upper Handguard, Gas Cylinder (#80). This will expose the Lower Handguard Lock (#40).
- Lower Handguard (#37), use a Flathead Screwdriver to lift the Lower Handguard Lock (#40) to the vertical position and slide it forward on the Barrel. Then slide the Lower Handguard (#37) forward and off the weapon.

Now you will need some of the tools and materials you obtained previously.

Remove the wood and plastic parts:
- Remove the stock by unscrewing the Buttstock (#15) from the Receiver (#62) and two flathead screws.
- Remove the Upper and Lower Handguards (#80 and #37)
- Rotate Handguard Latch (#81) to release the Upper Handguard/Gas Cylinder Assembly
- Lift and remove Handguard/Gas Cylinder Assembly (#80)
- Rotate Lower Handguard Lock (#40) to release the Lower Handguard
- Remove Lower Handguard (#37)
- Remove the Pistol Grip (#49) from the bottom of the Receiver (#62) by removing the Pistol Grip Screw (#51) located at the bottom of the Pistol Grip. The entire Pistol Grip Assembly, Part #s 49, 50, 51, 52, and 53, will become detached.

 *Note: The Pistol Grip Base (#52) is inside the Receiver (#62).*

Place the removed wooden and plastic parts off to the side, and you are now left with all the metal parts from the original AK47.

 *Note: When performing any drilling or grinding, be very careful, go slowly and use eye protection!*

Next, remove the Trigger Assembly, Safety Selector Stop Plate, and Magazine Catch:
- Place what is left of the rear portion of the demilitarized Receiver (#62) "bottom-up" in a vice and tighten until it is secure.
- You can remove the Magazine Catch (#43) from the Trigger Guard (#76) by tapping out the Magazine Catch Pin (#44). This will provide better access to the rivets you are trying to remove.

Chapter 2: Parts Preparation

- Remove the Trigger Guard (# 76) by grinding the heads off the rivets holding the Trigger Guard to the Receiver. A grinder, drill, or Dremel® is needed for this step.
- Grind off the Rear Trigger Guard Rivet (#78) and Front Trigger Guard Rivets (#77). If you have access to the rivet heads from inside the Receiver, it is best to grind them off from that side. Since you will be discarding the original Receiver damaging it is inconsequential.
- Grind what remains of the rivets holding the Safety Lever Stop (#71).
- Pry the Safety Lever Stop (#71) off the Trigger Guard (#76), and then pop what is left of the rivets through the Trigger Guard (#76).

 *Note: You must regrind the rivets several times in the process to avoid bending the metal of the trigger guard as you pop the rivets out. Try not to damage the Trigger Guard (#76) during disassembly because you will reuse it.*

…..And now the hard part….

Refer to Figure 5 below as the following steps are discussed. You have already removed the rivets that are easiest to extract (the Trigger Guard Rivets, labeled as #3). If present, the Trigger Pin and Hammer Pin, labeled as #7 below (parts #s 79 and 34 in the *AK47 Parts Diagram),* can be tapped out with a hammer and a punch.

This leaves the Front, and Rear Block Trunnions labeled as #s 1, 2, 4, 5, and 6.

 *Note: If you are not reasonably mechanically inclined, this is an excellent place to stop and go out and purchase a 100% US-made manufactured receiver and start the reassembly process.*
If not, we have to remove Front and Rear Block Trunnions, labeled as #s 1, 2, 4, 5, and 6.

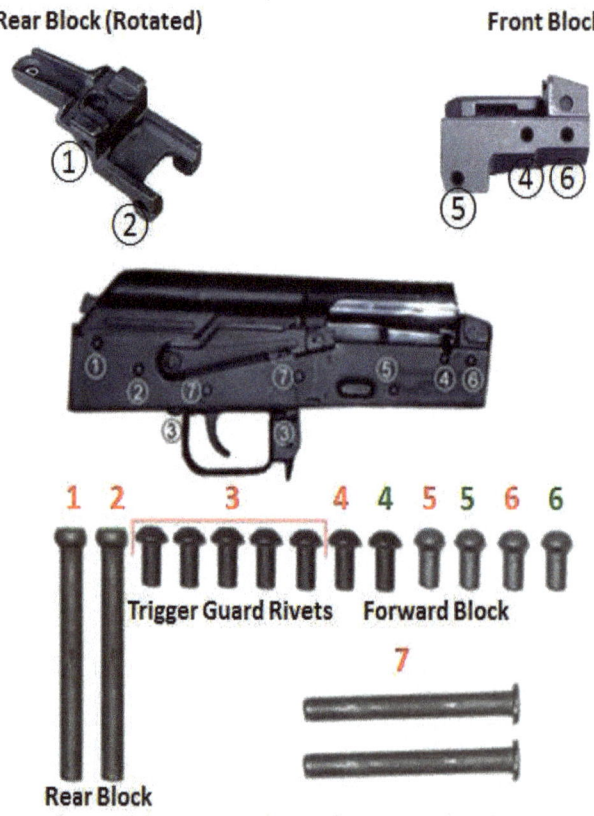

Figure 5, Receiver Rivet and Pin Locations

Chapter 2: Parts Preparation

You can press or drill out the Trunnion Pins. This process can be used on the Rear or Front Blocks. We will first go through the steps of drilling the pins out because it is the easiest method.

Remove the remains of the rear end of the Receiver from the Rear (or Front) Block:
- Grind the heads of Trunnion Pins off, then pry the off the Receiver from the Rear (or Front) Block.
- Use a file to remove any excess that remains of the pins protruding above the Rear (or Front) Block surface.

 *Note: A drill press is required for this process, and a securing mechanism (e.g., clamp or vice) is also needed to hold the Rear (or Front) Block rigid and level while drilling. A hand-held drill is not adequate for the task.*

Remove the Trunnion/Barrel Pins from the Rear (or Front) Block by drilling as follows:

- Secure the Rear (or Front) Block in the drill press with a vise/clamping device and ensure it is level on both the "X" and "Y" axis.
- Locate the center of the pin and drill a small pilot recess hole (approximately ¼ inch deep) using a #3 bit or smaller. Use lubrication oil as required while drilling.
- Remove the #3 bit, chuck in a #17 drill bit, and then drill entirely through the pin. Once through, remove the drill bit and chuck in a larger diameter bit until the pin is removed.

 *Note: This is a slow process, so don't get in a hurry. Otherwise, you may break the bit off. The pin may also start spinning as you drill. If so, stop drilling and use a pair of pliers to see if you can pull the pin out of the block.*

- Repeat the process to drill out the other pins.

 *Note: A sizeable hydraulic press is required for this process, and a securing mechanism (clamp or vice) is needed to hold the Rear/Front Block rigid and level while pressing. If you obtained the 12-ton press mentioned earlier, you are ready to start.*

 *Note: You may have to drill a hole in an aluminum block to align with and accommodate any rivet heads protruding from blocks while you press.*

Remove the Trunnion/Barrel Pins from the Rear (or Front) Block by pressing as follows:
- Secure the Rear (or Front) Block in the hydraulic press with a vise/clamping device and ensure it is level on both the "X" and "Y" axis.
- Brace the Rear (or Front) Block so that space can accommodate the Trunnion/Barrel Pin as it is pressed out.

Chapter 2: Parts Preparation

- Use a small pin (smaller than the Trunnion/Barrel Pin) to push the pin through the block. A hardened screwdriver shaft will suffice.
- Align the press over the pin to be pressed and extend the press until it touches.
- Slowly press down and observe the pin to verify it is moving.
- Pins can become seized in place with age and corrosion and be very hard to start moving. You may even hear a "pop" once they release.
- Once the pin breaks loose, pressing speed can be increased.
- Continue pressing until the pin falls free.

 *Note: The hydraulic press uses several tons of pressure, and if the items are misaligned, they are damaged or become projectiles.*

…..And now the tricky part….

 *Note: To minimize during barrel removal, apply paint remover to the top of the Barrel where it is exposed in the Front Block. Wipe off the paint residue and go over the Barrel with steel wool to remove any remaining specks.*

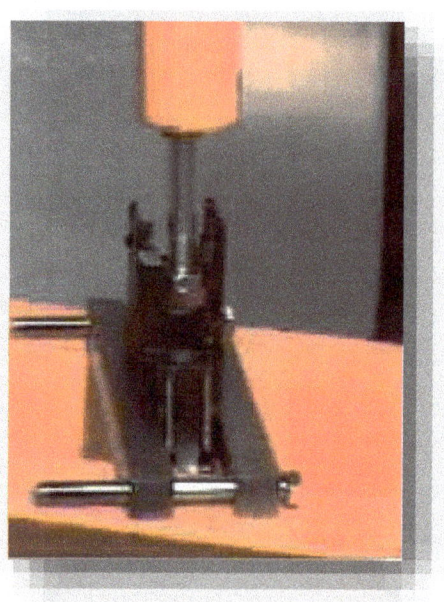

Remove the Barrel as follows:
- Place the Receiver Front Block into the hydraulic press and brace it so the Barrel hangs down.
- Use a couple of pieces of metal bar stock to support the mechanism while pressing. (see figure at right).
- Ensure the gas tube lock-down lever and the rear sight will not be damaged. The rear sight may need to be removed to prevent damage.
- Ensure there is adequate clearance below the Barrel for removal.
- Insert a penny (washer or other flat soft material which will protect the Barrel when removed) on top of the Barrel Chamber area.
- Insert a large push bar (a wrench socket or a large bolt with a couple of heavy nuts on the end will work well) on top of the penny and move the press head down until it contacts the push bar.
- Check to ensure that any area that could be damaged is clear.
- Slowly apply pressure to the push rod, ensuring alignment of the rod with the hydraulic press head.
- Apply additional pressure until the Barrel starts to move.
- When you see the penny in the Barrel Pin hole, stop barrel removal.
- Remove the Barrel/Front Block Assembly from the press area.

Chapter 2: Parts Preparation

 *Note: If you are reusing the Barrel, you must match mark the Barrel and the Front Receiver Block to provide alignment marks on the Barrel and Front Receiver Block for reinstallation purposes. White paint or a hammer and punch can be used to mark the Barrel/Front Receiver Block.*

- Once the match marks are in place, reinsert the Barrel assembly into the press.
- Slowly reapply pressure to the push rod, ensuring you are prepared to catch the Barrel when it falls.
- Remove the barrel/Front Block Assembly from the press area.

Cleaning Parts

Removing the Crud from Metal Parts

The old parts from your kit will likely be covered with gun grease (aka Cosmoline). *Cosmoline* is a type of preservative that was used to protect firearms in long-term storage. As you disassemble the rifle further, you start to find more and more of the Cosmoline. Not to worry, it is not difficult to remove. There are many ways to remove Cosmoline, and most of them work. You can use heat, chemicals, or a combination.

 *Note: Cosmoline is the genericized trademark for a common class of brown, wax-like petroleum-based corrosion inhibitors.*

Using the heat method, take the metal parts and place them on a tray in an oven on very low heat to melt them out. The tray will catch the grease as it drips out.

With the chemical method, use mineral spirits (or paint thinner) to remove the grease. You'll need a jug of mineral spirits, a pan or bucket, and some rags. Rubber gloves and an old toothbrush or paintbrush are handy to get into crevasses and prevent your hands from getting covered with chemicals and crud.

Place all the metal parts in a tub (or bucket) and pour the mineral spirits in. Only pour enough to cover most of the smaller pieces. The mineral spirits will break up the Cosmoline and make it easier to remove. After a few minutes, start picking out individual parts and cleaning them up. After cleaning, place them in a designated "clean" laydown area so they stay clean and are not misplaced. Newspaper or a 3' x 3' clean dry cloth will work for your laydown area and absorb the residual mineral spirits that drip off.

Chapter 2: Parts Preparation

 *Caution: Do not use gasoline. It is highly flammable, and it contains Benzene and other toxic chemicals.*

Removing the Wood from the Upper Handguard

 *Note: Damaging the wood when removing it from the Upper Handguard is easy to do. Follow the following instructions carefully when performing this task.*

Remove the wood from the Upper Handguard, Gas Cylinder (#80) as follows:

- Put the rear of the gas tube into a vise (Vise grips, Pliers, or a Crescent Wrench, but be careful not to damage the Gas Cylinder). In the figure at the right, you can see the blue masking tape protects the flat metal faces from damage.
- Then, with your hand, rotate the wood 180 degrees and pull it off.

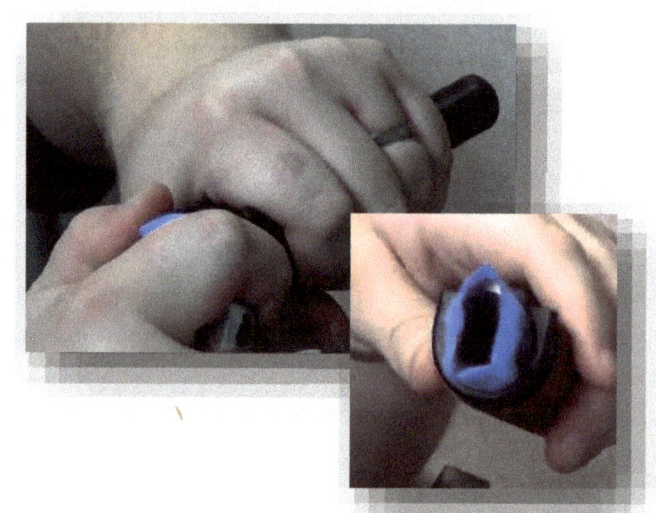

 *Note: I have included an excellent YouTube video link that demonstrates the procedure using your hands (http://www.youtube.com/watch?v=iyfcN7jLtQM)*

Refinishing the Wooden Parts

Clean and prepare the wood parts you intend to reuse as follows:
- Use Paint Stripper to remove old varnish following the directions on the can.
- After all the varnish is removed, use #60 grit sandpaper to clean up any significant scratches or blemishes.
- Use #150/220 grit sandpaper to smooth the finish and prepare it for staining.
- Use whatever stain you prefer (again, follow the directions on the can).
- Recommend Tung Oil vice wood stain for the final finish. Use a Tack cloth to wipe down the dried, stained wood surfaces before applying Tung Oil with a clean rag.
- Allow the Tung Oil to dry overnight, then use fine steel wool to dull the surface, then use a Tack cloth to wipe down for another Tung Oil coat.

- Repeat as required until you see the Tung Oil no longer penetrating into the wood (approximately five coats usually will get you to this point).
- You can use a varnish (or polyurethane) to seal it all up (again, follow the directions on the can).

Refinishing the Metal Parts

The original AK47 is likely either a blued or a Parkerized black phosphate finish. I do not go into the details to refinish the metal parts because there are many options (e.g., Parkerizing, bluing, electroplating, etc.), and each metal finish requires a slightly different process for preparing the metal.

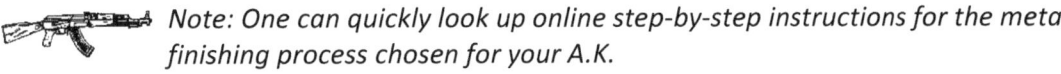 *Note: One can quickly look up online step-by-step instructions for the metal finishing process chosen for your A.K.*

The metal refinishing process is not complicated, but it can be long, arduous, and expensive. Therefore, I have decided to omit it from this document. However, I am not abandoning you in the middle of the task.

A brief internet search will yield several websites with detailed instructions (and possibly videos) describing the various processes for refinishing metal gun parts. To limit search returns, I recommend deciding what type of finish you want for AK47 before performing the internet search.

Chapter 3: The Receiver

Below is an outline of what you will learn in this chapter.

At this point, your parts are clean, and you are deciding what old parts you will replace with the new US-made parts and which parts you will fabricate yourself.
- ✓ Deciding what parts to discard.
- ✓ Building your Receiver.

What to Discard

At this point, you should have decided which of the original AK47 parts to discard. Also, as discussed in the first chapter, you can only have a maximum of ten (10) imported parts in the final version of your AK47 to meet Federal Firearms Laws. If confused, re-read Chapter 1. See regulatory excerpts listed below:

The G.C.A., 18 U.S.C. § 922(r), specifically states the following:

*Note: It shall be **unlawful for any person to assemble from imported parts any semiautomatic rifle or any shotgun which is identical to any rifle or shotgun prohibited from importation** under the...[G.C.A.]...Section 925(d)(3).as not being particularly suitable for or readily adaptable to sporting purposes ....*

Note: Also, 27 C.F.R. § 478.39 states:

*... (a) **No person shall assemble a semiautomatic rifle or any shotgun using more than 10 of the imported parts listed in paragraph (c)** of this section if the assembled firearm is prohibited from importation under section 925(d)(3) as not being particularly suitable for or readily adaptable to sporting purposes ....*

Chapter 3: The Receiver

 *Note: If you still have not performed this task, I recommend the following link to help you in this process (http://www.gunwiki.net/Gunwiki/BuildAkVerifyCompliance).*

If the website above does not help or is not available, here are some suggestions:

Replace the following at a minimum with US-made parts:
- Receiver and Trigger assembly (Reasons: The Receiver is unusable, and the original Full-Auto Trigger assembly is illegal)
- Barrel (Reason: It is likely to be worn and corroded and near end of life)
- Magazine (Reason: It counts under the regulations, and it is not difficult to comply)

If you choose to keep the Barrel and Magazines as original (from the list above), then replace all of the furniture (#s 15, 37, and 80) and Pistol Grip Assembly (#s 49, 50,51, 52,53) with U.S. parts. Some people do this anyway because they may want a more tactical design, hunting or sportsman's style, or just don't like the looks of the original rifle.

Also, one of the things that, in a way, help is if any parts are missing from your original AK47 parts kit or if any are unserviceable parts, then replacing those parts will contribute to your US-made parts count.

To Buy or Build Your Receiver

You must replace your Receiver (#62) with a US-made part, and it can either be *milled* or *stamped*. Milled Receivers are strong, will not twist, and should last many years of shooting. On the other hand, they also cost more, are heavy, have fewer stock options, and few parts kits are available for the milled receivers.

Stamped Receivers are much more common and are easy to build yourself. They also can be strong. However, if poorly constructed, they can also twist and warp with stress, and rivets, welds, and screws can work loose.

A Federal Firearms Transaction must be performed if you buy a finished manufactured receiver (either milled or stamped). In the eyes of the Federal Government, the receiver is the firearm. Receivers are subject to all firearms laws, with regulations on sales across state lines, ownership by felons, shipping regulations, etc. The rest of the rifle is just parts under the law. However, if you build your receiver from stock metal or pre-stamped flat plates, no Federal Firearms Transaction processing is required. Therefore, you can legally build (and own) an unregistered AK47 from parts for yourself; provided you also meet the following requirements:
- the Barrel is 16" or longer, and the overall length is more than 27";
- the rifle(s)/receiver(s) are not being built with the intent of reselling them;
- all state and local laws permit you to build your rifle;
- the receiver being built is semiautomatic only (i.e., no machineguns); and
- (For pistol builds only), the receiver cannot accept a Buttstock of any kind, and there can be no vertical foregrip.

Chapter 3: The Receiver

Building Your Receiver

Once again, there are several requirements for building your receiver. Making your receiver involves taking a receiver flat, bending it into the squared-off U-shape, spot welding the rails in place, and heat treating the completed receiver to add strength and durability. See figure at right.

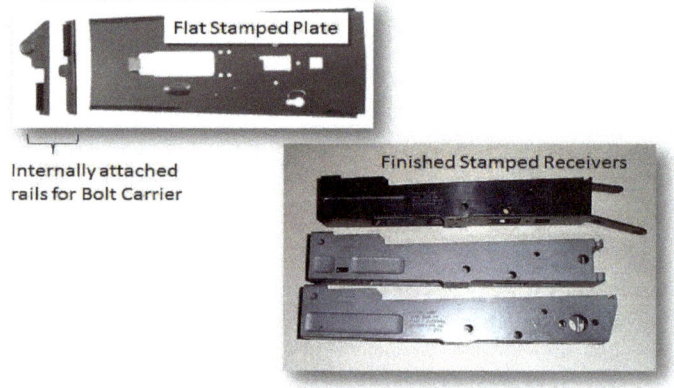

If you really want to bend your receiver from a flat, a separate custom-made (or purchased) bending jig fixture is required (see figure at left). You will start with a standard flat receiver and use the bending jig fixture and a hydraulic press to create the basic shape. After pressing the basic shape, the rails are bent over with a hammer and soft metal block. The trigger pin holes are drilled after bending.

After folding the receiver, it's time to add rails, extractor, and center pin. A spot welder is the preferred method for attaching the side rails, but you can also use rivets, screws, or tack welds to attach the rails. Whichever method you use, be sure to heat treat your new receiver after bending and attaching rails. After hardening, your receiver will last for years.

As you can see, building your receiver from a stamped flat is quite extensive (building from a plain piece of sheet metal is even more difficult), and I recommend you save the task for later after you have built a few AK47s using manufactured receivers.

The following instructions assume you have purchased a US-made 100% (or 80%) manufactured Receiver and are starting from that point.

Chapter 4: Putting it All Back Together

Chapter 4: Putting it All Back Together

Below is an outline of what you will learn in this chapter.

Your Receiver is reassembled, and parts are on hand and ready. It is time to reassemble the rifle.
- ✓ Reinstalling the Barrel and the Rear Sight Base.
- ✓ Reinstalling the remaining Barrel Assemblies.
- ✓ Installing the Receiver (Trunnion) Blocks.
- ✓ Installing the Trigger Guard Assembly.
- ✓ Installing the Trigger Assembly.
- ✓ Reassembling the weapon.

Reassembly of the Major Assemblies

Reinstalling the Barrel

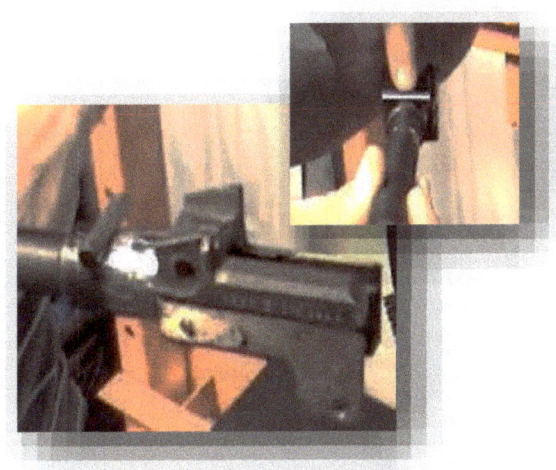

Note: If the Front-End (Trunnion) Block is already mounted in the Receiver, pressing the Barrel back into place requires either angle iron, or a simple fixture to hold the Front-End Receiver (Trunnion) Block while the Barrel is pushed back into place.

Reinstall the Barrel as follows:
- With Barrel partially inserted and the Rear Sight Base (#57) removed, lay the Barrel Pin in the groove on top of the Barrel and ensure it aligns evenly with the Front-End Receiver (Trunnion) Block (see figures at right).

Chapter 4: Putting it all Back Together

 *Note: Before you press your Barrel, ensure the mating surfaces are smooth. If not, sand them smooth, but do not remove too much metal or cause the Barrel to become out-of-round.*

 *Note: Before pressing, place a solid plate under the Front-End Receiver (Trunnion) Block and a soft metal spacer between the tip of the Barrel and the hydraulic press to prevent damage.*

- Place the Front-End Receiver (Trunnion) Block into the hydraulic press and brace it so that the Barrel points up.
- Check to ensure that any area that could be damaged is clear.
- Slowly apply pressure to the top of the Barrel while ensuring alignment of the Barrel with the hydraulic press head.

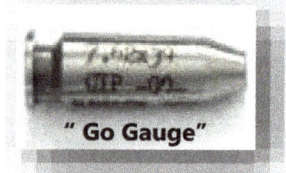

" Go Gauge"

- Apply additional pressure until the Barrel starts to move.
- Check for headspace and adjust the Barrel using a stripped Rifle Bolt and a headspace gauge (see Go/NoGo gauge, at right) until proper headspace is achieved.
- With Barrel installed, remove the Barrel/Front Block Assembly from the press area.

Reinstalling the Remaining Barrel Assemblies

Reinstall the Rear Sight Base (#57) as follows:

- Ensure the Barrel surfaces are pre-lubricated with machine oil and slide Rear Sight Base (#57) onto the Barrel.
- Align the Rear Sight Base (#57) with the top of the Front-End Receiver (Trunnion) Block and ensure there is adequate clearance below the Barrel for removal.
- Place the assembly in the bar stock fixture (see figure at right)
- Move the press head down until it contacts the top of the assembly.
- Check to ensure that any area that could be damaged is clear.

Chapter 4: Putting it all Back Together

- Slowly apply pressure to the assembly, ensuring alignment of the Front-End Receiver (Trunnion) Block with the Rear Sight Base (#57).
- Continue to apply additional pressure until the Front-End Receiver (Trunnion) Block aligns with the back edge of the Rear Sight Base (#57) (see figure at right).
- Remove the Barrel/Front Block/Rear Sight Assembly from the press area.

Reinstall other Barrel Parts as follows:
- Reinstall the Lower Handguard Clamp Assembly (#s 38 & 40) and lock it down.

 *Note: If this is not done before the Front Sight Base (#57) is installed, you will have to remove and reinstall the Front Sight Base.*

- Reinstall the Gas Port Block (#31) by first clamping the Gas Cylinder (#80) into the Rear Sight Base (#57).
- Ensure the Barrel surfaces are pre-lubricated with machine oil and slide the Gas Port Block (#31) onto the Barrel.
- Verify that the Rear Sight Base (#57), Gas Cylinder (#80), and Gas Port Block (#31) are all aligned, then place into the press (see figure at right).
- Move the press head down until it contacts the top of the assembly.
- Check to ensure that any area that could be damaged is clear.
- Slowly apply pressure to the assembly, ensuring alignment until the Gas Cylinder (#80) covers the holes of the Gas Port Block (#31).
- Reinstall the Front Sight Base (#25) by first covering the Barrel mating surfaces are pre-lubricated with machine oil, and slide Front Sight Base (#25) onto the end of the Barrel.
- Verify the Front Sight Base (#25) is aligned with Rear Sight Base (#57).
  Place Barrel Assembly into the hydraulic press with Front Sight Base (#25) pointing up and use a 5/8"(or larger) socket as a press bar and press the sight onto the Barrel.
- Drill out the pin holes for the Gas Port Block (#31).
- Using a small, tap the pins into Gas Port Block (#31).

Chapter 4: Putting it all Back Together

 *Note: Wait until you test fire the rifle to Drill out the pin holes and install the pins for Front Sight Base (#25). Some adjustment of the Front Sight may still be required.*

Reassembly of the Receiver

Installing the Receiver (Trunnion) Blocks

Trunnion Block Riveting Jig

Installing the Receiver (Trunnion) Blocks are some of the more difficult steps in the process (aside from bending the receiver) mainly because a specialty tool is required to press the rivets (see figure at right) or a pair of Bolt Cutters (shown below right), a Propane Torch can be used with the Bolt Cutter method to ensure better rivet deformation. Using a rivet tool and press is the preferred and more professional method.

Assuming you have a Rivet Tool, the holes are pre-drilled in the Receiver, Propane Touch, and you have the U.S.–made rivets (foreign rivets can often be substandard); other tools you might need are Insulated Pliers, Ball Peen Hammer, Leather Safety Gloves, and

Reinstall the Front-End Receiver (Trunnion) Block as follows:

- Verify that rivets will fit easily into the holes.

 *Note: If you are using a manufactured Receiver, the holes should align, and you can place Rivets (or a proper-sized drill bit) in the holes you are not presently riveting to maintain alignment. If you*

Bolt Cutter Riveting Tool

manufacture your receiver, you may need to clamp the Trunnion Block in place and drill your holes first. If you predrilled your holes (in a homemade receiver) and they are not aligning, you may have "egg-shaped" your holes (this procedure is not recommended).

 *Note: You may want to start with the lower two (2) rivets in the Front-End (Barrel Trunnion) and the Trigger Guard rivets since they are the most accessible.*

Bolt Cutter Method (Propane Torch is optional):
- Pick up the first rivet with a pair of insulated pliers (if using a Torch).
- Using Propane Touch, heat the rivet shank (not the head) until Red.

Chapter 4: Putting it all Back Together

- Using the pliers, install the rivet in the first hole.
- Place the Bolt Cutter Rivet Tool on the top of the button head and slowly close the jaws. Little pressure is required since the rivet is hot (if you did not heat the rivet, more pressure might be needed (see figure at right).
- Press the rivet head all the way down until it touches the receiver crushing the rivet shank until flat.
- Allow for cooling (if heated) and repeat for the rest of the rivets.

Bolt Cutter Riveting Tool *Shown Clamped*

 *Note: The purpose is to distort (flatten) the shank of the rivet at the bottom so that the rivet does not come out of the hole. Do one on the left side of the receiver, then one on the right.*

 *Note: Ensure the receiver or Front-End Receiver (Trunnion) Block does not move and the holes remain aligned during each rivet installation.*

 *Note: There are two (2) types of rivets, flat and swell-necked. The flat rivets insert into the front two (2) holes of the Front-End Receiver (Trunnion) Block, and the swell-necked goes in the back hole.*

 *Note: Some rivets are of the wrong size. Therefore, care should be taken to ensure rivets are the correct size; rivets which too long will become misshapen, and too short will not adequately flatten and hence will not hold in place.*

Rivet Tool Method (preferred):
- Start with the middle hole (of the three holes) for alignment purposes and insert a rivet into the hole to be riveted. Insert rivets/drill bits in other holes to maintain overall alignment.
- Place the receiver in the rivet tool and align the tool as shown at right.
- Place the Rivet Tool on the top of the button head and slowly press with a hydraulic press.
- Press the rivet head all the way down until it touches the receiver.
- Repeat for the other two (2) rivets

Front Trunnion Block Being Press Riveted

Chapter 4: Putting it all Back Together

Note: When installing the Rear-End (Trunnion) Block with rivets, the type of rivets and where you install them will depend on whether you are building an AK-47 with a folding stock or normal stock. In either case, use the hydraulic press to crush these rivets into place.

Note: Before riveting the Trigger Guard Assembly (#s 76 and 71) in place, use two (2) small (#8 or smaller) machine threaded screws/bolts (with nuts and washers) to firmly hold the Trigger Guard in place. Use one (1) hole in front and one (1) back, and leave the other holes empty to install rivets in. Then try to insert an empty Magazine (#42) in the magazine well. If it does not fit, loosen and adjust the screws/bolts as required. This pre-alignment step will avoid rivet rework on the Trigger Guard later.

Trigger Guard Riveting Jig

Reinstall the Trigger Guard Assembly *(#s 76 and 71)* as follows:
- Once the Trigger Guard Assembly is aligned so as not to interfere with the Magazine (#42), place Receiver (#62) into the jig (see *Trigger Guard Riveting Jig* at right).
- The slightly shorter rivets go in back, and the longer rivets go in front because the longer rivets hold an extra layer of sheet metal in place (Safety Lever Stop, part #71).
- Insert Receiver (#62) as shown at right and align the hydraulic press head with *Trigger Guard Riveting Jig* and slowly press with a hydraulic press.
- Press the rivet head all the way down until it touches the receiver.
- Repeat the process for the other rivets.
- Take the Receiver (#62) out of the jig and remove the machine screws/bolts previously installed for alignment purposes and reinsert them into the Receiver (#62) *Trigger Guard Riveting Jig*.
- Repeat the process for the last two (2) rivets.

Trunnion Guard Being Press

Installing the Trigger Assembly

Note: Installing a US-made trigger group should be easier, and many AK47 enthusiasts agree that it also performs better than the original trigger assembly in semiautomatic

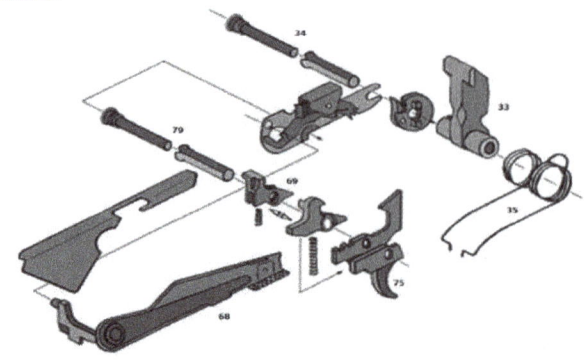

Chapter 4: Putting it all Back Together

mode. See exploded *US-made semiautomatic typical Trigger Assembly figure at right*.

 Note: *Figure 6, at the right, differs slightly from the diagram provided at the end of the text. Hopefully, one of the two properly represents your AK47 Trigger Assembly.*

Install the Trigger Assembly as follows:
- First, put the Hammer Spring (#35) on the Hammer (#33) and wrap the arms around the flat part of the hammer.
- Slide it into place between the Receiver rails and push its pin (#36) through the receiver to hold the Hammer (#33) in place.
- Assemble the Trigger (#75) and Disconnector (#69) with the spring from your parts kit.

 Note: *Your parts kit (A.K. variant) may not look exactly like this figure. In this case, follow the kit instructions or seek further information online.*

 On many *US-made parts kits, there is a round sleeve to hold the parts together to allow easier installation. If not, manually hold the parts together and drop them into the receiver so you can pin them.*

- Drop the Hammer Spring (#35) arms down and hook the hammer on both sides.
- Reinstall the Safety Lever (#68) by pulling the trigger and inserting Safety Lever in the rotated up position perpendicular to the Receiver (#62); once inserted, rotate down until the "Safe" position.
- After assembling your rifle, test the Trigger Assembly by holding down the Trigger (#75) and cycling the bolt. Observe the gap to see if the hammer is falling as the trigger is pulled.

 Note: *Some US-made triggers are adjustable to allow the draw weight to change based on user preference.*

Final Rifle Reassembly

Reassembly is the disassembly process in reverse. Start with the *furniture (*wood and plastic parts).

Reinstall wood and plastic parts as follows:
- Reinstall the stock by screwing the Buttstock (#15) to the Receiver (#62), using two flathead screws.
- Reinstall the Lower and Upper Handguards (#37 and 80)
- Reinstall Lower Handguard (#37), rear end first, and Rotate Lower Handguard Lock (#40) to lock the Lower Handguard in place.

Chapter 4: Putting it all Back Together

- Insert the end into the Gas Port Block (#31), then drop the Upper Handguard/Gas Cylinder Assembly into place.
- Adjust Handguard Latch (#81) as required to accommodate placement.
- Rotate Handguard Latch (#81) and lock it in place.
- Reinstall the Pistol Grip (#49) to the bottom of the Receiver (#62) by attaching the Pistol Grip Screw (#51) located at the bottom of the Pistol Grip.

Reassemble the remainder of the weapon as follows:

- Slide Bolt Carrier (#8) onto receiver rails; the Hammer (#33) may need to be depressed.
- If your kit has one, reinstall the Cleaning Rod (#16).
- Slide Recoil Spring Assembly (part #s 65, 66, and 67) back into the Gas Cylinder and push forward until it clears the rear notch and releases. Ensure the Recoil Spring Guide (#65) catches in the notch.
- Reinstall the Receiver Cover (#63) and ensure the Recoil Spring Guide (#65) pops out the back of the Reinstall Receiver Cover (#63).

Your AK47 is now assembled. Clean, lubricate and test fire.

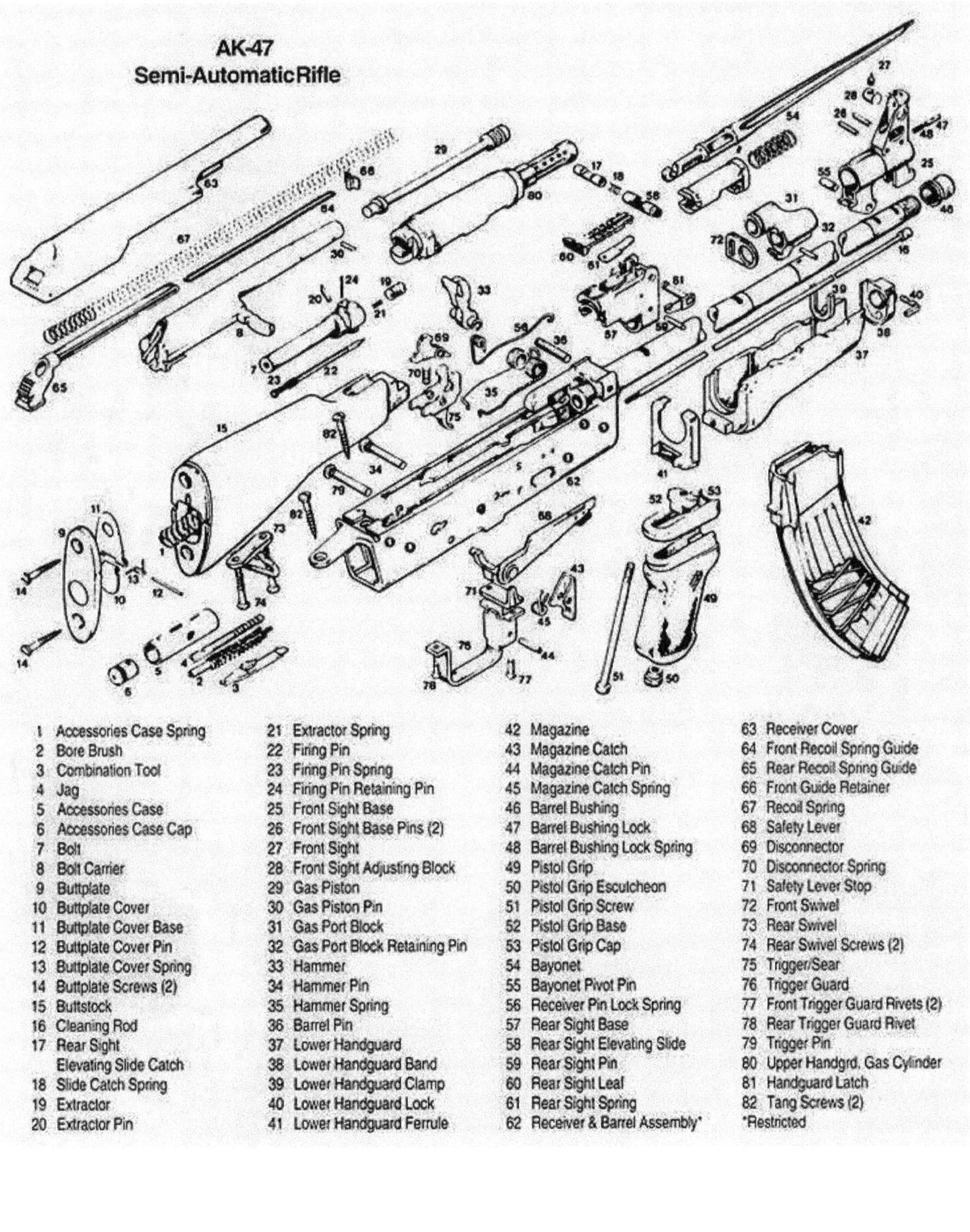

Chapter 4: Putting it all Back Together

AK-47 Semi-Automatic Rifle

#	Part	#	Part	#	Part	#	Part
1	Accessories Case Spring	21	Extractor Spring	42	Magazine	63	Receiver Cover
2	Bore Brush	22	Firing Pin	43	Magazine Catch	64	Front Recoil Spring Guide
3	Combination Tool	23	Firing Pin Spring	44	Magazine Catch Pin	65	Rear Recoil Spring Guide
4	Jag	24	Firing Pin Retaining Pin	45	Magazine Catch Spring	66	Front Guide Retainer
5	Accessories Case	25	Front Sight Base	46	Barrel Bushing	67	Recoil Spring
6	Accessories Case Cap	26	Front Sight Base Pins (2)	47	Barrel Bushing Lock	68	Safety Lever
7	Bolt	27	Front Sight	48	Barrel Bushing Lock Spring	69	Disconnector
8	Bolt Carrier	28	Front Sight Adjusting Block	49	Pistol Grip	70	Disconnector Spring
9	Buttplate	29	Gas Piston	50	Pistol Grip Escutcheon	71	Safety Lever Stop
10	Buttplate Cover	30	Gas Piston Pin	51	Pistol Grip Screw	72	Front Swivel
11	Buttplate Cover Base	31	Gas Port Block	52	Pistol Grip Base	73	Rear Swivel
12	Buttplate Cover Pin	32	Gas Port Block Retaining Pin	53	Pistol Grip Cap	74	Rear Swivel Screws (2)
13	Buttplate Cover Spring	33	Hammer	54	Bayonet	75	Trigger/Sear
14	Buttplate Screws (2)	34	Hammer Pin	55	Bayonet Pivot Pin	76	Trigger Guard
15	Buttstock	35	Hammer Spring	56	Receiver Pin Lock Spring	77	Front Trigger Guard Rivets (2)
16	Cleaning Rod	36	Barrel Pin	57	Rear Sight Base	78	Rear Trigger Guard Rivet
17	Rear Sight Elevating Slide Catch	37	Lower Handguard	58	Rear Sight Elevating Slide	79	Trigger Pin
		38	Lower Handguard Band	59	Rear Sight Pin	80	Upper Handgrd, Gas Cylinder
18	Slide Catch Spring	39	Lower Handguard Clamp	60	Rear Sight Leaf	81	Handguard Latch
19	Extractor	40	Lower Handguard Lock	61	Rear Sight Spring	82	Tang Screws (2)
20	Extractor Pin	41	Lower Handguard Ferrule	62	Receiver & Barrel Assembly*		*Restricted

Figure 7, AK47 Parts Diagram

www.ingramcontent.com/pod-product-compliance
Lightning Source LLC
LaVergne TN
LVHW071630130825
818582LV00031B/3051